who are you?

ten days to discovering "who you are"

who are you?

ovo gharoro

Cover and Page design by four-nine-zero design.
www.fourninezerodesign.co.uk

Illustrations by Joseph Oyem.
www.ojamstar.deviantart.com

Order this book online at www.trafford.com/07-2926
or email orders@trafford.com

Most Trafford titles are also available at major online book retailers.

Note for Librarians: A cataloguing record for this book is available from Library and Archives Canada at www.collectionscanada.ca/amicus/index-e.html

ISBN: 978-1-4251-6374-7

We at Trafford believe that it is the responsibility of us all, as both individuals and corporations, to make choices that are environmentally and socially sound. You, in turn, are supporting this responsible conduct each time you purchase a Trafford book, or make use of our publishing services. To find out how you are helping, please visit www.trafford.com/responsiblepublishing.html

Our mission is to efficiently provide the world's finest, most comprehensive book publishing service, enabling every author to experience success. To find out how to publish your book, your way, and have it available worldwide, visit us online at www.trafford.com/10510

www.trafford.com

North America & international
toll-free: 1 888 232 4444 (USA & Canada)
phone: 250 383 6864 • fax: 250 383 6804 • email: info@trafford.com

The United Kingdom & Europe
phone: +44 (0)1865 722 113 • local rate: 0845 230 9601
facsimile: +44 (0)1865 722 868 • email: info.uk@trafford.com

10 9 8 7 6 5 4 3 2

contents

acknowledgements

It took many years of private research to produce this book, but without the input of many who are dear to me and some kind people I met on the journey called life, it would never have reached the standard that it is now. Of these many, I would like to thank a few without whose input this book would still be a dream.

Chukwuka and Azuka Oyem for their constant encouragement. Many times I felt like giving up, but these brothers and their family have been a blessing and constant support.

Donna Ojegba and Oge Ilozue, whose advice and input could not have gone unnoticed. Although I have only known them a short time, Oge's mentorship and Donna's friendship were very instrumental to the development of this book. I have transformed many of our conversations into words in this book. Thank you for listening to me and making me think.

Bola Folami, Stacey Bryan, Bukki Oriola, Nneka Ene, Ore Bajomo, Abigail Adenaike, and Joseph Oyem, whose input, no matter how small, helped to make this book happen. Just a quick word of encouragement from you, or just listening to what I had to say on the topic, helped me to have come this far.

Minister Abay Aromire and Pastor Ade D'Almeida–your insight and counsel shaped this book into what it is now.

Mr Bright, a mentor when I needed one, a friend when I was in need, and a father figure even when I thought I could live without one. I am where I am now because of people like you, and I say, thank you.

Aunt Charlotte Coker–this book could not be the quality that it is now without you. Your mentoring and insight have not only shaped this book and the marketing plan round it. They have also shaped me.

I can't forget two of the most important people without whom this book would not be here: my mother, Mrs E. D. Gharoro, and one of my closest friends, Gloria Yamson.

My mother's resilience to go on and the sacrifices that she made are the only things that allow me to be here today. I would not be where I am now if not for my mother.

Gloria's contributions in our conversations can't be put into words. You are truly a special and amazing person. My only wish is that I can contribute as much to your life as you have to mine. Your influence on this book was as invaluable as your presence in my life.

Finally, I would like to acknowledge my pastor and my greatest mentors, the people who changed my life the most: Pastor Matthew Ashimolowo, Dr Mike Murdock, Dr Myles Munroe, and the Holy Spirit (my Greatest Mentor). Your sermons have changed many lives–mine is just one of them.

dedication

I would like to dedicate this book to everyone who helped make me *who I am,* every friend and every foe. I would also like to dedicate this book to the person without whom this book would not exist, a man of great wisdom, encouragement, and my first inspiration, my father, Mr A. C. Gharoro. The death of my father while I was young and what he contributed to the world that he left behind was my first inspiration to write. He could bring order to any situation in a matter of minutes, and his writing, though not famous, inspired those near and far.

I would also like to dedicate this book to my mother, Mrs E. D. Gharoro, a pile of strength in any right. She has had a profound influence on the way I think.

foreword

I always say that "you must know something about everything". This book gives great insight on everything you need to know about identifying, empowering, and developing yourself. It is full of basic but profound knowledge and tips on success, living a better life, and overcoming obstacles.

It is no doubt a fact that everything in life rises and falls on leadership. However, true leadership begins within ourselves and this is what Ovo tries to achieve through this book–developing the leader within.

One thing to note is that by developing the leader within, you are improving yourself. This is exactly what the book offers with its step-by-step guide on "finding the real you" and what to do with yourself afterwards. Whilst reading this book's manuscript, I found out that the daily guide takes you through a process where you can evaluate your progress against your expectations.

This book will empower you to clearly understand the words of Ben Franklin:

> 'By improving yourself, the world is made better. Be not afraid of growing too slowly. Be only afraid of standing still. Forget your mistakes, but remember what they taught you.'

This book will not just help you grow but give you insight into the faith and mind of the author, Ovo Gharoro. Ovo is undoubtedly an inspiration to many, including myself, and this is why I recommend that every aspiring world leader read this book. It will not just empower you but open your eyes to your ability to live by faith and not by means. In this book, Ovo takes us through his personal experience and how some key events have shaped his life, I can testify that applying some of those keys to my life has helped me grow.

This book is different from many other inspirational writings. Hence, as you read this book and apply the principles that Ovo shares, you will discover that you are on the way to another dimension of growth and progress in every area of your life.

It is a must read for every individual who wants to go higher!

Ambassador Dayo Israel

British Red Cross Humanitarian Citizen Ambassador
Young General Assembly Special Representative to United Nations Meetings

day one:
introduction

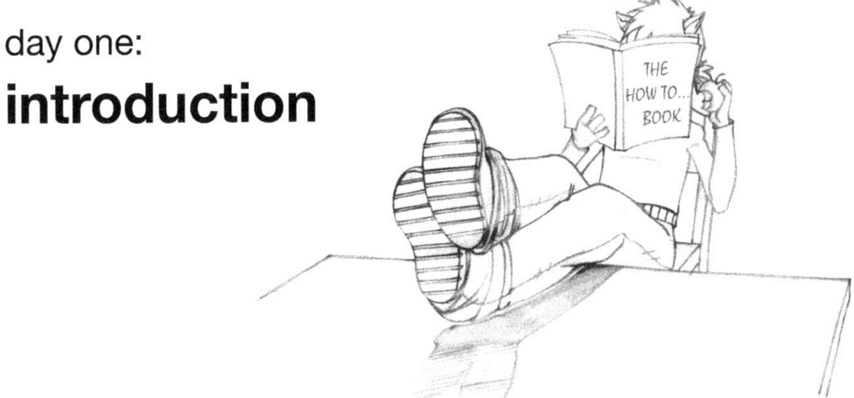

Thank you for picking up this book. Over the next ten days, I hope to take you through a process that will change your life forever. It will allow you to start *living life* and fully enjoy the beauty of your life in the world we live in today.

This book is divided into three main sections. These sections are designed to make this journey clear and understandable because, for many people, the journey is not clear, and it is certainly not understandable. The sections are as follows:

- **how to discover *who you are.***
- **obstacles to discovering *who you are.***
- **what to do next.**

This book is meant to be completed in ten days. I have chosen ten days because it represents the biblical number of increase. I pray that you increase as you read and progress on this journey over the next ten days.

Yes, the book is written to be read in ten days, but that is only a guideline. You could read it in five days or you could read it in twenty. Take it at the pace that best suits you. It is a very personal journey, and for that reason I want you to

make it as personal as possible.

This book works better as a guide and for that reason I ask that you go on the journey with someone. This could be a parent, a mentor or a friend. It will give you a chance to discuss what you discover daily with them and hold you both accountable for completing the journey. The important thing to remember is that you pick who you go on this journey with and not the other way round – it is your choice.

obstacles to discovering *who you are*

In case you are still not aware of what the journey is, it is the process of discovering *who you are.* The title of the book must have been a dead give-away. However, this book does not stop at just discovering *who you are.* I also want to equip you to face the challenges that come with that discovery and advise you on what to do next.

Before you begin this journey, you may be asking yourself, "Why must I go on this journey to begin with?" I will answer this question by giving you some **definitions** of terms used in this book. Then I will explain **why it is important to discover *who you are*** and **why I am qualified to write this book.** There. You are clear on our pre-journey, so let us begin.

definitions

I am going to begin by defining a few terms. Some terms you may be familiar with, others not so much. You may even think you know what I am referring to when I first use them, but please take the time to understand them in their context. The terms are *success, "who you are,"* and *living life.*

success

Ask ten people how they define success and you are sure to hear ten different definitions. Many people define success by the amount of money they have, but ask some of the richest people in the world and they will let you know that money doesn't mean success. Money is a by-product of success. After all, it is possible for you to inherit all your money. Does that make you successful?

What is success? Success can be a verb (succeed) or a noun. **The definition of the verb succeed is the accomplishment of a task/goal that one has set out for themselves.**

the definition of the verb succeed is the accomplishment of a task/goal that one has set out for themselves.

By definition, you are successful when you are full of success.

If your goal is to get an "A" on your exam and you achieve it, that is your success. If it is to score a goal in a football match and you achieve it, that is your success. You set a goal, and you achieve it.

The noun success refers to an end point when you have arrived at your final destination. This destination is unique for each individual. Hence, the term purpose comes into play.

> the noun, success, refers to an end point. when you have arrived or when you have reached your final destination.

The only person who can tell when you have arrived is you, and no one else. Until you get to that place, you are simply successful.

"who you are"

Your purpose is determined by *who you are.* Without knowledge of *who you are,* you cannot accurately say what you are meant to do or achieve on this earth. Therefore, you can't determine your *success* without knowing *who you are.*

***The question "Who are you?"* is not asking for your name. It is asking for your identity, the embodiment of everything that makes up you. *Who you are* is your dream, your vision, your abilities, and your attitude, your differences from everyone else.** What makes you significant? What makes you stand out in a crowd?

> the question *"who are you?"* is not asking for your name. it is asking for your identity, the embodiment of everything that makes up you. *who you are* is your dream, your vision, your abilities, and your attitude, your differences from everyone else.

It is what you were created to achieve, what you are predestined to do, the one thing you do better than anyone else.

I use the word *destined* and *destiny* loosely because we can influence the outcome of our destinies. However, what we cannot influence is what we are, or are not naturally good at. Knowing our natural abilities aids in our purpose.

Some people are naturally fast runners, Michael Johnson and Maurice Green, for example. Others are great singers and musicians like Mozart and Whitney Houston. Sure, these people had to work to develop their natural gifts, but their gifts were still natural. They had the potential for greatness at the very start.

living life

What is *living life?* ***Living life*** **is a term I use to describe when you know your purpose (or** ***who you are*****) and live life with the aim of achieving that purpose, with the aim of becoming a** ***success.***

living life is a term i use to describe when one knows their purpose (or *who they are*) and lives a life with the aim of achieving that purpose, with the aim of becoming a success.

When you live life without purpose, you have not yet begun to live life. You may not yet agree with this, but as many people who have discovered their purpose will tell you, nothing you did prior to this discovery matters. Everything that you did before you discover *who you are* will often feel insignificant.

Now that I have defined my terms, I can begin to explain to you why it is important to discover *who you are.*

why it is important to discover *who you are*

Purpose is knowing what you were meant to do with your life and then going ahead and getting it. That is one of my mission statements and values.

purpose is knowing what you were meant to do with your life and then going ahead and getting it.

Many of the people who I come into contact with believe that in your youth you are not meant to know what you will do with your life. A lot of people in the world believe that it is OK to be lost, confused, or not know where you are heading with your life until you are much older. I am going to paint a different picture because I do not think they are right.

Many of the most successful people today and in the past share something in common. They made up their minds early on in life as to where they wanted to be, what they wanted to do or what path they wanted to take.

Tiger Woods, the best golfer in the world, began to play golf at the age of two.[i] Warren Buffett, the greatest investor and the richest man in the world (as of March 2008), started investing when he was eleven.[ii] David Beckham, one of the most famous football players in the world, can trace his career in football back to when he was just fourteen when he signed with Manchester United.[iii] Michael Jackson, one of the most famous pop stars and the self-crowned "King of Pop" began his singing career at the age of seven.[iv]

David was anointed king of Israel when he was a teenager.[v] Joseph, who became the second most powerful man in Egypt, saw his family bow down to him in a dream when he was seventeen.[vi] Samuel, one of the greatest prophets in the Bible, heard God for the first time when he was but a boy.[vii] Jesus, the Son of God, went about His Father's business when he was only twelve.[viii]

The greatest and the most famous started their journeys early. Why do some people feel they have to wait to start theirs? Do you feel like you have to wait?

---

i *Amateur Career, Career, Wikipedia, http://en.wikipedia.org/wiki/Tiger_woods*

ii *Overview, Wikipedia, http://en.wikipedia.org/wiki/Warren_Buffett*

iii *Childhood and early career, Wikipedia, http://en.wikipedia.org/wiki/David_Beckham*

iv *Michael Jackson, Wikipedia, http://en.wikipedia.org/wiki/Michael_Jackson*

v *1 Samuel 16, The Holy Bible*

vi *Genesis 37, The Holy Bible*

vii *1 Samuel 3, The Holy Bible*

viii *Luke 2, The Holy Bible*

Maybe you do not want to be known as a great person in history. No one says that you will or will not be great if you decide to follow your purpose. There are many people without whom the world as we know it would not be the same, but they are not famous.

Just to prove my point, do you know who invented the Internet? As you will agree, whoever invented the Internet is a very important person but not as famous as Henry Ford or Thomas Edison. Who invented the mobile phone or the hair dryer?

> purpose does not mean famous and it does not mean rich.

Purpose does not mean fame, and it does not mean riches. Many rich and famous people are not necessarily living according to their purpose. I say this because a lot of them are not happy. They live very destructive lives and are still chasing something to bring them happiness. How else do you explain the high divorce rate among celebrities or the need for some of them to adopt children from third-world countries? How do you explain the mental breakdowns, depression, drug abuse, and suicide attempts?

Why chase after happiness in the wrong places, in the wrong things, or in the wrong people? If you want to be completely happy with your life, then you need to know *who you are.* Before I found out who I am, I also fell victim to looking in the wrong places–relationships, friends, popularity, and so on.

Nothing that is outside your purpose will ever fulfil you. It is like drinking salt-water to satisfy your thirst. The more you drink, the thirstier you become. Fulfilment comes from achieving your purpose. It comes from becoming a *success.*

> nothing that is outside of your purpose will ever fulfil you.

If you decide to live a life without purpose, you will look back at your life with regret. Having a life with purpose does not mean that you can't do the things you enjoy. In fact, I now do more of the things I enjoy more often than at any other time in my life.

> fulfilment comes from achieving your purpose.

I am asking you to make this decision to start the journey of discovering *who you are* and your purpose. It is the second most important decision you will need to make in your life (I will tell you the first later).

When you don't know *who you are,* you will likely find yourself

- **experiencing constant failure.**
- **always moving with the crowd with every decision you make.**
- **doing the right thing but not necessarily the right thing for you.**
- **lacking provision in what you are trying to achieve.**
- **frustrated because things seem ten times harder for you than they do for other people.**

You may already be experiencing a life like this, but it is not too late to change that. Make the decision and begin the journey.

why I qualify to write this book

Before you pick a guide book for a trip, you must know that the author has been through the journey himself and has guided people to that end. I am such a person.

When I was sixteen years old, my dad died and my life changed completely. Before this time, I could say that my life was pretty insignificant. I did some pretty amazing things but nothing that mattered. I am the kind of person who, if you tell me I am not good at something, will work hard just to prove you wrong, and I have done that with many things. However, nothing I accomplished really mattered.

When my dad died, I suddenly realised that I had to take life seriously. As you could imagine, it was a confusing and frustrating time for me. My dad was not ill all the time, and his health had never been an issue. One day, he just had a stroke. Two weeks later, he was gone.

I became very violent, but I guess my teachers understood because I never got kicked out of school, not even after dislocating someone's shoulder. It may also have had something to do with the fact that I was brilliant in maths and science (something that someone once told me I was terrible at).

At seventeen, I started reading the Bible regularly. I discovered that people in the Bible seemed to discover *who they were* at the age of seventeen. I wanted to know *who I was* mainly because I wanted to know why some events in my life had happened.

I went through a process of discovering my purpose. I realised that my experience was not unique. Many people have been through the same process.

I worked as a part-time teacher, and for this reason I had a lot of exposure to young people. So many of them were at a point in their lives where they had to make important decisions, and I guided them through the process.

In my short time on this earth, I have been privileged to guide a number of people through the process of discovering *who they are.* No journeys are identical, but no journey is unique because they all work under the same principles. I have mastered these principles and will explain them in this book.

We have come to the end of the pre-journey and the end of Day One. Tomorrow you begin the process of discovering *who you are.* Tonight I want you to reflect on the reasons why you want to take this journey. This is an important journey, but if you have not made up your mind to take it, spend some time reflecting on whether this journey is for you.

something for you to do:

I want you to be completely honest in this section. This is your future and your life, so your honesty is greatly needed.

Am I ready to start this journey? (Yes/No)

____

Why do I want to go on this journey?

____

____

____

____

____

____

____

____

____

____

____

____

____

I, ____________________________, commit to the journey of discovering *who I am.* I take this decision seriously, and I am willing to spend the next nine days in complete reflection of what I am about to learn in this book.

Signed ______________________________ Date _________

day summary

- The definition of the verb ***succeed*** is the accomplishment of a task or goal that you have set out for yourself.
- The noun ***success*** refers to an end point.
- The question *"Who are you?"* is not asking for your name. It is asking for your identity, the embodiment of everything that makes you up. Who you are is your dream, your vision, your abilities, and your attitude, everything that makes you up, your points of difference from everyone else.
- ***Living life*** is a term I use to describe when you know your purpose (or who you are) and live life with the aim of achieving that purpose, with the aim of becoming a success.
- The greatest and the most famous started their journeys early. Why do you feel you have to wait to start yours?
- Nothing that is outside of your purpose will ever fulfil you.

If you don't know *who you are,* you are not yet living life.

day two:
searching inside yourself

how to discover *who you are*

We now know why we should discover *who we are.* The next step is to actually discover it. Over the next three days, we will discuss the principles that have helped me and countless others discover *who they are.* I have divided these principles into three parts:

- **searching inside yourself**
- **searching outside yourself**
- **turning to God**

For those of you who are not religious, don't worry this is not a religious book. However I can't talk about purpose without referring to God or a spiritual belief system. The two topics are so closely knitted.

Let's begin the journey with searching inside yourself.

searching inside yourself

Most journeys of self-discovery begin with the individual, and with that in mind, this will be no different.

I find that in discovering *who you are,* there are two things you need to look at inside you. The first is **your emotions,** and the second is your **gifts.**

your emotions

With your emotions, there are three questions you need to answer:

- **what makes you angry?**
- **whose pain do you feel?**
- **whose joy do you celebrate?**

what makes you angry?

Who makes you angry? What situation makes you angry? What do people do to annoy you? What irritates you the most about this world and the people in it?

Have you ever heard someone say that one person's rubbish is another person's treasure? What that statement also implies is that someone's problems could be another's heaven or, better still, solutions. In other words, if something is not a problem to you, there is no reason you should attempt to solve it.

> only when a problem angers you will you recognise it as a problem and become eligible to solve it.

what angers you the most? that is something you were meant to change.

Only when a problem angers you will you recognise it as a problem and become eligible to solve it. In other words, only when a problem angers you will you be motivated to solve the problem.

You simply can't solve a problem until it angers you. If you are failing to solve a problem that doesn't anger you, it is because you are not the one meant to solve that problem. **What angers you the most? That is something you were meant to change.**

I once sat on a bus on my way to Stratford (in London) coming from my home in Chadwell Heath, when I noticed a bee buzzing around two windows up from me. A woman and her daughter were seated there. When the woman saw the bee, she immediately tried to kill it with her shoe, but her daughter warned her that she might break the window. She stopped immediately and changed seats.

She saw the problem, and it made her angry (maybe not angry enough). Because of her fear of the consequences of solving the problem however, she withdrew and fled. She still saw a problem, and she moved away and didn't solve the problem. She stopped herself from solving it because of what her daughter said.

Then a man came and sat near the window with the bee. On seeing the bee, he fled. He also saw a problem but was too afraid to solve it. It didn't make him angry to see the bee. He was just scared–clearly not the right person for the job.

Another man came in, saw the bee, and killed it. He saw a problem; it angered him; he solved it without thinking.

What problems do you solve without thinking? If you have to think about it, you may not be the right person for the job, but do not let other people's opinions stop you from doing what comes naturally to you. If that woman were not with her daughter, she would have solved the problem. Don't let other people rob you of discovering *who you are* or the rewards of being *who you are.*

> don't let people rob you of discovering *who you are* or the rewards of being *who you are.*

If you love something, you will stand up for it and oppose those who are against it. I love wisdom and oppose ignorance. Curing ignorance has become my calling.

A teacher should hate the lack of education in people. A mentor should hate the mistakes in a protégé. Therefore, the mentor tries to correct and change them.

A problem leads to anger; anger leads to solving the problem; solving the problem is your purpose.

something for you to do:

What things annoy you?

At home?

____

____

____

At work/school?

In the world?

What sorts of people annoy you?

At home?

At work/school?

In the world?

Why do these things make you angry?

What can you do about it?

____

____

____

____

____

whose pain do you feel?

When you watch the news or a film or even hear a story, whose tears make you want to cry? Who makes you want to rescue them? What pain do you feel?

Have you ever wondered why when someone drops out of school, some friends support the decision to drop out while others do not? Does supporting the decision to drop out make you less of a friend than someone who urges the person to stay in school?

It's not as if you are being a bad friend by supporting the decision to drop out. Instead, you are just being a *now friend*, that is not thinking about tomorrow and how that might affect your friendship. Some friends don't care about your tomorrow while others do. I will say this again, being a *now friend* doesn't make you a bad friend. I am a *now friend* to certain people, and I have a lot of now friends too. Not everyone you meet is meant to be in your future. Not everyone you meet will try to pull out *who you are.*

> not everyone you meet will try and pull out *who you are.*

Tragedy or disaster can often lead to you doing something to ease someone else's pain. **Great dreams are often birthed from pain,** your pain or the pain you see in someone else.

> great dreams are often birthed from pain, your pain or the pain you see someone else in.

A model in the US was involved in an accident that disfigured her face. This almost destroyed her as her whole life revolved around the beauty of her face. After some therapy, she decided to have plastic surgery to reconstruct her face. Later, she returned to modelling and is now helping people who have been in disfiguring accidents to get back on their feet. Her accident gave her life a purpose that had not been there before.

Pain is not always a bad thing. I used to feel sorry for people who were in great pain. A relative or spouse died; they were in a serious accident; they or a loved one had a terminal disease. I am not saying that it is bad to feel sad for them but that in most cases the pain they feel gives birth to a purpose.

For example, when I lost my father, pain was there, but it helped me screw my head on the right way (or perhaps tighter). I became more aware of wisdom and ways of attaining success that would have otherwise passed me by. **It was the circumstances that I was in that gave me**

drive. My determination to succeed at all costs was born from the pain I was feeling.

> it was the circumstances that i was in that gave me drive. my determination to succeed at all costs was born from the pain i was feeling.

Pain can birth purpose, so listen to your pain and the pain of others around you.

something for you to do:

What things make you sad in your school or job? What things would you like to change?

____

____

____

____

____

____

What events in your life have really made you sad?

____

____

____

____

____

____

What things in the world today make you sad?

____

whose joy do you celebrate?

What makes you happy? Who makes you happy? What event or success in someone else's life brings a smile to your face?

It is often difficult to be happy for other people when they succeed while you fail, but that is not what I am talking about. Something about the joy someone else feels when they succeed pulls you in so that you too become happy and share in their happiness.

As an artist, I find that I become interested in the work of other artists but only in the sphere of my own art. I am excited to see something that I cannot do or that I would like to do. It interests me to read books on what I am led to believe is my calling. I am interested in the writing style of other writers, in the information they give, and in critiques of their work. I break-dance, and when I see someone who can break-dance well, I am always eager to see or meet and talk with that person. I am a poet, and reading the great poetry of others inspires me to write great poetry. When I walk into an organised function or attend a well-planned event, I feel happy, and it brings me joy.

I often hear about the success or wisdom of a close friend, but this doesn't make me jealous. It simply makes me eager to do more myself. If you don't enjoy or feel led to do something, then you will not want to do more of it unless of course, you have a problem...

Seeing a building being built can make some people happy–maybe they were called to be architects or civil engineers. Or maybe it is art that makes you happy–you could be an art dealer.

Something about someone else's happiness is making you happy. What is it? Only by relating can you ever truly be a part of something. If something brings you joy, maybe you were meant to be a part of it. So think about it. Whose joy do you celebrate?

something for you to do:

Whose happiness makes you happy? Some people are happy carrying babies or watching children laugh. How about you?

____

____

____

____

What events in the lives of your friends make you happy the most?

____

____

____

____

Why?

____

____

____

____

your gifts

Who you are can be identified by the gifts and talents that you possess. You will always have the purpose to do something that you have a gift for and are passionate about–singing, dancing, football, maths, accounting, physics, whatever.

In order for you to find your gifts, you may have to try many things. The aim is to find the things that best suit you, the ones that you love and are good at.

> sometimes you love something but you are not good at it; that is not your gift – you simply admire the gift and the people who have them.

Sometimes you love something but you are not good at it. That is not your gift. You simply admire the gift and the people who have it. Some people, like myself, have a love for football but can't play the sport well because it is not my gift.

You may have a talent for something that has not yet been tapped into properly. You will never know if you are good at something unless you try it. Michael Jordan, whom a lot of people hail as the king of basketball, was cut from the team. His coach from school told him that he would never play professional basketball.

> Born in Brooklyn, New York, Michael Jordan … was cut from the varsity basketball team during his sophomore year because at 5 ft 9 in (1.75 m) he was deemed underdeveloped, but over the summer he grew four inches (10 cm) and practiced even harder. Over his next two seasons, he averaged 25 points per game. He began focusing on basketball, practicing every morning before school with his high school varsity coach. In his senior season at Laney High, Jordan averaged a triple-double: 29.2 points, 11.6 rebounds, and 10.1 assists. He was selected to the McDonald's All-American Team as a senior.[i]

There are things that you are naturally good at, and there are things that you have to work at. One or both of them may be your calling in life.

> there are things that you are naturally good at and there are things that you have to work at; both of them maybe your calling in life.

something for you to do:

What talents and gifts do you have?

____

____

____

____

i *Early years, Michael Jordan, Wikipedia, http://en.wikipedia.org/wiki/michael_jordan#early_years*

Which of them are you the best at or really love doing?

____

____

____

What is it about this gift or talent that excites you?

____

____

____

And so ends Day Two. Today you looked at your emotions–what makes you angry, sad, or happy. Please take the time to fill in those blanks if you have not already done so.

day summary

- There are three parts to discovering *who you are*: searching inside yourself; searching outside yourself, and turning to God.
- When searching inside yourself, you should look at your emotions and your gifts.
- With your emotions, answer these questions:

  What makes me angry?
  Whose pain do I feel?
  Whose joy do I celebrate?

- Work to understand your gifts.

  Your purpose will always have something to do with your talents.

day three:
searching outside yourself

I hope that you have identified some things about yourself from the previous day that you didn't know. Day Three takes us outside ourselves. There are three major aspects that I will invite you to look at when addressing this search:

- **your mentors**
- **your friends**
- **your interests and conversations**

your mentors

In discovering *who you are,* it is important that you find out what you are interested in. You will only succeed at what you have an obsession or a passion for. It is easier to make something an obsession when you like or love doing it. What interests you? Is it wisdom, music, relationships, current affairs, movies, art, dancing?

The best way to find out what your interests are is to find a mentor.

A mentor is someone to look up to, someone you connect with, whose advice you follow, whom you respect, and who is constantly looking to do what is best for you (although at times you may not see it). This is someone who is already where you want to be or has passed through something that you are going through now. A mentor is a lot like a teacher but is interested in passing on wisdom rather than just information.

> a mentor is someone who you look up to, who you connect with, whose advice you follow, who you respect and who is constantly looking to do what is best for you (although at times you don't see it).

find a mentor

A lot of people take their parents as their first mentors, but over time you get to choose your mentor. Sometimes they choose you. I took my father as my mentor when I saw the way he would look at a chaotic situation and bring order to it with just a few words. We shared attributes that connected us in a very special way.

When looking for a mentor, look for someone you respect, someone you connect with, someone who has gone through something you are going through, or someone who is where you want to be.

> a mentor can't teach you to fly if he himself can't fly.

If you want to be in a position of leadership, you have to know, respect, and follow the advice of someone who is–not just a

finding a mentor

leader but–a great leader. As the saying goes,"A defeated boxer can only teach you how to be a defeated boxer." A mentor can teach you to fly only if he or she can fly.

> a defeated boxer can only teach you how to be a defeated boxer.

Finding a mentor places you as a protégé to that person. The intriguing thing about the word protégé is that it is (French) from the past participle of protéger, to protect. It also refers to someone whose welfare, training, or career is promoted by an influential person–your mentor. That is a mentor's job–to help and protect you.

Once you have found a mentor you connect with, understand why you connect with that person. I have a few questions for you to answer to help you understand your connection.

something for you to do:

Do you have a mentor?

____

Who is your mentor?

____

What is it about this person that you respect or look up to?

____

____

____

____

What position do you want to be in?

____

____

Do you know anyone in that position now?

____

____

Who is in that position?

____

____

What is it about this position that excites you?

____

____

____

____

____

your friends

When looking at the area of your friends, there are two questions that I want you to ask yourself:

- **whom do I draw to me?**
- **what am I most recognised for?**

Whom do I draw to me?

Have you ever noticed how, no matter where you go, after a while the same sort of people gravitate towards you of their own free will? It is amazing to see that when a crowd of people meet for the first time, people who are dressed the same, who talk the same, who are the same race or skin colour come together.

> leaders pull leaders in, rappers pull rappers in, and footballers pull footballers in. your personality shines.

This same theory applies whenever you meet new people. **Your personality screams out to people with similar personalities. Leaders pull in leaders, rappers pull in rappers, and footballers pull in footballers. Your personality shines,** but it isn't something that is easily noticed.

Look at your closest friends. Ask yourself why you are close to them. It is interesting to see the reason why we chose certain people as our friends.

Do you notice that you are always going out with

the same person, just with a different face or name? I found that my entire grouping of close friends reminded me of a close friend I used to have. You are pulled to the same type of people, and they are pulled to you. However, what is important is recognising why!

What about them pulls you in? Is it their leadership skills or perhaps their love of organisation? Something about them connects with you, and you need to figure out why.

something for you to do:

Describe your friends.

____

____

____

____

Why do you think they enjoy being with you?

____

____

____

____

Ask them and find out why they do.

____

____

____

____

Why do you think the people you go out with are attracted to you (I am not referring to physical attraction here)?

____

Ask them and find out why.

what am I most known for?

Everyone was meant to stand out. If you don't stand out, there is something wrong.

When people want to have a conversation about something or have a question on a certain topic, do they come to you at times? If an event is going on, do people think to call you because they feel you would be the best or one of the best people to handle or take part in such an event? If not, you need to change that.

Everyone is meant to have their name synonymous with something. When I say Nelson Mandela, you think President of South Africa, freedom fighter, very old guy, been in prison for a very long time, and so on. When I say David Beckham, you think football, Real Madrid, LA Galaxy, strange fashion sense, always in the media, used to be in Manchester United.

what am I most known for?

what do people think about when they see you?

Different people make you think of different things. What do people think about when they see you?

I once heard it said that if you are thirty and over and you have not yet been asked for interviews of some kind (for something positive, not negative), you are doing something wrong.

A few years ago at a youth conference, there was a "break-dance clash". It was going on at a different part of the conference from where I was. I was enjoying a quiet game of chess, when some people came up to me. They called to me and asked if I knew there was a break-dance freestyle going on.

They did this because they felt that I should be there, that I was good enough or talented enough to take part. They recognised something in me and for that reason pulled me aside.

What do you find yourself constantly doing? The ability to stay calm, happy, or even joyful in a hard, chaotic, or sad time is in itself a gift. Not many people can do that, and this may be what makes you special and different.

Please go through the following questions.

something for you to do:

What do people most know you for?

Ask your friends and people in your school or workplace. What do they say?

What would you like to be known for?

your interests and conversations

I know today has been a long and taxing day, but please keep going. You are nearly finished. This section asks you two more questions and requires some self-reflection:

- **what books interest you the most?**
- **what conversations attract you?**
- **recognise *who you are.***

What books interest you the most?

The topics that interest you the most are clues to what you are meant to be or do. They are clues to *who you are*. When I didn't know what my calling was, it was very interesting to read wabout wisdom, purpose, and success. Books like *The Power and Purpose of God's Glory* by Dr Myles Munroe really interested and inspired me. They helped me on the path to discovering *who I am* and are still helping me.

something for you to do:

What types of books do you like to read?

What is it about these books that attracts you?

What would you like to be known for?

---

what conversations attract you?

When people talk, certain conversations pull you in. For instance, talking about wisdom and purpose gets me excited and fired up, while someone talking about computer software and programming excites my friend. What conversations do you find yourself joining in the most? Even when it comes to gossip, some gossip interests you and other gossip doesn't. Why?

when people talk, certain conversations pull you in.

This is because you are automatically drawn to your interests and your wisdom (that is, what you know) whether it be fashion, cars, movies, films, relationships, comedy, or current affairs. Some people know about football statistics and talk about them all the time because that is their wisdom.

You can only succeed at something you love, know about, and are confident in.

I used to feel left out when people were talking about football and I could not contribute, so I went home and started watching all the games on television, even learning the names of a few players and their positions. To me this was a huge effort, and I thought at least I would be able to add a little to their conversations. Despite my efforts, I still could not contribute because football was not my wisdom.

What do you know about? What are you good at? What do you talk about? This is your wisdom. **Your wisdom is part of *who you are.***

something for you to do:

What gossip do you like to hear about?

___

___

___

What news in the media interests you?

___

___

___

What do you enjoy the most at school or work and why?

___

___

___

___

___

___

What do you and your friends talk about the most?

___

___

___

___

___

___

___

recognise who you are

When having conversations with people, talk about your talents and gifts. Listen to what they have to say about you. What do people say that you are good at? The words of others can be very revealing.

> the words of others can be very revealing about what you are good at and what you are not.

When listening to people talk about your talents, purpose, and gifts, the most important person to listen to is your mentor. Your mentor recognises things in you that you may not be able to see, and your mentor tells you because he or she sees in you aspects of himself or herself and knows how to recognise your talents. Remember, your mentor has been through what you yourself are going through.

I have a friend whom I admire for the way she commands authority and respect and the way she handles responsibility. When I refused to run for a position on the committee of my society, she confronted me and asked why, almost demanding that I run for a position. She saw the possibility for leadership in me that even I didn't see. "Greatness will recognise greatness." Look for the person who recognises greatness in you–your mentor.

Other people see in you things you don't see in yourself. People sometimes recognise *who you are* before you do. They see your faults and your gifts. And by people, I mean the right people. **What do these people see in you?**

You need to use their words as mirrors to recognise *who you are* and also change your faults. Because finding out *who you are* (your purpose) will take your whole life, this process of recognition and correction is a constant process.

Words are mirrors. They either show *who you are,* who the person is you are talking to, your future; your past, or your present.

However, when words or people speak of your past failures and mishaps, you need to stop them. It is the past! Stop talking about it! You're a changed person.

something for you to do:

What have people said about you?

____

____

____

What has your mentor said about you?

____

____

____

Who do you think you are?

____

____

____

If you can't answer the first two questions now, ask some people. Ask them what they feel you are meant to do with your life and what they think you represent. Ask them what makes you different and special. Finally, ask them why they think this of you.

We got to the end of Day Three. I know it might have been a bit of a struggle, but you made it. Sit back and reflect on what you have learnt about the world around you, and we will kick off tomorrow with "Turning to God".

day summary

- There are three parts to discovering *who you are*: searching inside yourself, searching outside yourself, and turning to God.
- When searching outside yourself, you should look at your mentors, friends, interests, and conversations.
- With your mentors, answer these questions:

  Who is my mentor?
  Why is this person my mentor?

- With your friends, answer these questions:

  Whom do I draw to me?
  What am I most known for?

- With your interests and conversations, answer these questions:

  What books interest me the most?
  What conversations attract me?
  What is my identity?

day four:

turning to God

> God is not a last resort, he is the first.

God is not a last resort. He is the first, so do not let the fact that I put this part last make you feel that way. I chose this day to talk about God because I recognise that some part of you may not believe in God and that talk of turning to God may offend you.

Some people use God to explain the unexplainable. To an extent, I will do that today. Even so, this is the most important chapter of this book.

We'll start by looking at two areas:

- **what lesson is life trying to teach you?**
- **the greatest mentor**

what lesson is life trying to teach you?

In life, sometimes it seems as if we have seen more than our share of pain or lessons in one thing. We have been hurt constantly by a thing or we have had something so radically change our lives that it seems unfair to us and the rest of the world.

In the Bible, we read about Moses, an Egyptian Prince of Hebrew birth who was destined to lead his people into the "Promised Land". In order for him to lead them, he first had to travel a vast wilderness, a desert.

I have often wondered why he ran away to seek refuge in the land of the Midian. He went away from his people after he realised his Hebrew heritage, but still had a passion to rescue them from their bondage.

He was a Prince of Egypt and clearly had the power to get them out of Egypt, but what could he do next?

He would have to lead them to the "Promised Land" through the wilderness. He was raised in the palace, so he certainly developed leadership skills. However, he knew nothing of the wilderness. He still needed to learn about that.

He also needed to learn the proper way to achieve his

goals. For example, he killed an Egyptian whom he saw beating a Hebrew. After that, even his fellow Hebrew brothers did not trust him. He could not lead his people if they didn't trust him.

Hence, he was exiled to the wilderness and stayed there for forty years. In the wilderness, he learnt about survival, serving God, and the right way to do things. After forty years, he was ready to lead.

Life is trying to prepare you for your purpose through its lessons.

life is trying to prepare you for your purpose through its lessons.

You need to let yourself mature.

I once heard a pastor say, "The harder the lessons, the greater the calling".

something for you to do:

If life is your teacher, what lesson do you think it is teaching you?

____

____

____

What kinds of things always seem to happen to you?

____

____

Why do these things happen to you?

the greatest mentor

If you want to know exactly how a product is meant to work, there are three things that you can do. You could read the manual. You could ask the manufacturer. You could get a good technician to explain it to you.

God, along with the Holy Spirit and Jesus Christ, created you. They are your manufacturers. The Holy Spirit knows you through and through and can be asked about anything pertaining to *who you are.*

the greatest mentor

"Before I formed thee in the belly I knew thee; and before thou camest forth out of the womb I sanctified thee, and ordained thee a prophet unto the nations". (Jeremiah 1:5, KJV Bible)

The manual is the Bible–**B**asic **I**nformation **B**efore **L**eaving **E**arth–read it. The Bible covers any and every question you may have concerning your life and your purpose, but the only problem is that, like most manuals, it is hard to understand on your own.

god, along with the holy spirit and jesus christ, created you. they are your manufacturers. the holy spirit knows you through and through and can be asked about anything pertaining to *who you are.*

To understand the Bible completely, you need someone to teach you–the Holy Spirit, who is your mentor, helper and counsellor. The Holy Spirit knows you, so in everything you do, pray to Him and He will guide you in all things. That is the purpose for which He is here.

On the other hand, you can ask a technician. Technicians are people like me, born to help others discover *who they are.* They may be your pastor, your father, your teacher, your mentor, someone in a position to explain to you the things you don't understand.

I used to say that there is nothing more important than discovering your purpose. I learnt that no matter how far you go trying to find your purpose, you can never completely understand or walk in it without God (or to be more precise, the Holy Spirit).

i learnt that no matter how far you go trying to find your purpose, you can never completely understand or walk in it without god (or to be more precise, the holy spirit).

The Holy Spirit designed you and assigned you your purpose.

It is for you to discover and understand, not make or decide. **You could search all your life and finally discover your purpose when you are old and grey, but wouldn't it be easier just to ask your creator?**

Imagine, for instance, that you are a new software programme or smart device, but you didn't know what you were designed to do. You could try all your life doing different things until one day you come across what you were meant to do. Or you could call the developers (for example, Microsoft) and ask them about your purpose.

---

something for you to do:

Pray and ask for the Holy Spirit to guide you to discover who you are.

To compensate for the long day yesterday, I have granted you a short day today–yes, this is the end of the day. Tomorrow we begin to look at the obstacles to discovering *who you are.* As I said, though, today is the most important day, so I will say a prayer with you.

> *Heavenly Father, I thank You for the life of Your child. I thank You for giving everyone the opportunity to know You better. I thank You for giving everyone the chance to discover who they are. Holy Spirit, open their hearts and speak to them. Open their spiritual ears that they may hear from you. Fill them with Your mercy and wisdom. Grant them insight into Your heart and Your desire for their lives. Show them, Lord, who they are. Amen.*

day summary

- There are three parts to discovering *who you are*: searching inside yourself, searching outside yourself, and turning to God.
- When turning to God, you should look at what life and your Greatest Mentor are trying to teach you.
- When looking at what lessons life is trying to teach you, answer these questions:

  What keeps happening to me?
  What experiences do I keep going through?

- With your Greatest Mentor, remember:

  He is the Holy Spirit.
  He knows you inside and out. If you ever need a "cheat" to finding out your purpose, this is it.

say this prayer with me:

Father, as I begin today my path to discovering who I am, help me, Lord. My purpose is very important to You. It is the reason You made me. Help me to find it, and help me to fulfil it.

Amen.

day five:

the enemy within part 1

obstacles to discovering *who you are*

Discovering *who you are* is a process, and although the title of this book suggests that it can be done in ten days, it takes longer to fully understand it. It took me years to get from a feeling to a mission statement and then a full-blown vision. I am still developing individual tasks and objectives on a daily basis.

in ten days, you will get to a point where you have the right mindset and are asking the right questions to get you there.

In ten days, you will get to a point where you have the right mindset and are asking the right questions to get you there. In fact, you might be there now, but don't put down the book yet.

This next section covers the main reasons why people never complete the journey. I don't just want you to start this journey but get to the end. Therefore, I am first going to tell you what challenges you will encounter and then how to get past them.

The obstacles you will face can be broken down into two main areas which we will cover over the next three days:

- **the enemy within**
- **people, places, situations, and things**

the enemy within

If you have not already guessed, the enemy within refers to you. I have always found that the greatest challenge you face when carrying out any change to yourself is yourself.

I have identified several areas that are relevant to you. Remember, not every journey is identical, so you may find that one or two do not apply:

obstacles to discovering *who you are*

- **disbelief in yourself**
- **unwillingness to solve the problems that most infuriate you**
- **procrastination**
- **fear of failure**
- **past failures**
- **satisfaction in what you have already accomplished**

Disbelief in yourself

People don't discover *who they are* because they can't believe that someone as "little" as they are could be great. A lot of the time, the greatest opposition to your vision and discovering *who you are* is yourself.

> people don't discover who they are because they can't believe that someone as "little" as they are could be great. a lot of the time, the greatest opposition to your vision and discovering who you are is yourself.

Think about it. People who drink, smoke, or overeat can only change this by fighting themselves.

Fighting yourself is one of the hardest things to do. The same can be said about fighting the way you see yourself.

The way you view yourself is very important regarding your successes in life. If you see yourself as a failure, it should be no surprise when you fail.

Have you ever tried to do something and told yourself that you were going to fail even before you started? How did you do?

> no winners tell themselves before they go into battle that they are going to lose and then expect to come back victorious and great in battle. it is unheard of.

No winners tell themselves before they go into battle that they are going to lose and then expect to come back victorious and great in battle. It is unheard of. No matter how bad you are at something or how much better someone else is at it, you have to begin with the belief that you can come out on top.

In my second year at university, I started a tutoring agency called University Tutors (UT). However I almost didn't do it.

The idea of starting a business at my young age was frightening. **The problem that I didn't believe that I could do it.** I didn't believe in my abilities as a teacher and a leader. In the past, I had often fallen victim to this, but this time I prevailed. Even the thought of writing this book was scary, to say the very least, and as with everything else in my life, it almost didn't happen.

Disbelief in self destroys self. It makes you a failure even before you begin. Don't just *do* something. *Believe* that you can do it.

Unwillingness to solve the problems that most infuriate you

> disbelief in self destroys self.

Recall the story from Day Two about the bee on the bus. That is a case of someone not solving the problem that most infuriated her. I have already narrated this story, so I won't do it again. You can flip back to remind yourself of it.

Recall that the woman who sat in the seat was infuriated by the problem and would have solved it if not for her daughter. **Her daughter brought out a fear in her that solving the problem may create a greater problem by damaging the bus. She stopped herself because of fear.** In case you didn't know, most glass used in vehicles today is made from fibre-glass. A shoe would not be able to break it, but she didn't think it through. She didn't solve her problem, deciding to move instead.

The next person ran from the problem. If he didn't see it as a problem he would have stayed where he was instead of moving. He was scared of the problem and ran.

The last man saw the problem for what it was and solved it.

These are three categories of people who saw a problem that infuriated them, but all reacted differently. The key difference among them was **fear.**

Sometimes we are afraid of a problem that we are meant to solve. Something frightens us, so we don't solve the problem.

> sometimes we are afraid of a problem which we are meant to solve.

Every venture I go into is solving a problem. By not solving problems, I am not realising the full potential within myself. What if Nelson Mandela had never solved the problem that most infuriated him? South Africans might still be oppressed today.

What problem are you not solving that you should be? "If it itches, scratch it." **What itch aren't you scratching?**

> "if it itches, scratch it." what itch aren't you scratching?

procrastination

Procrastination is "the art of keeping up with yesterday".

> procrastination is "the art of keeping up with yesterday".

If you are trying your best to keep up with yesterday, how do you expect to plan for today, let alone tomorrow? Without planning you are shooting an arrow and praying that it will hit something by chance.

> now if you are trying your best to keep up with yesterday, how then do you expect to plan for today, let alone tomorrow?

With everything in life, you need to plan. If you want to succeed completely with every endeavour you partake in, then you must plan it out properly. "If you fail to plan, you plan to fail".

When you procrastinate, things only get harder. Every time you do not do something that you were meant to do, task only becomes more difficult.

This, however, this is not the worst of it. Imagine that you put off doing something that pertained to your future and thereby missed an important opportunity. Sometimes opportunities come once in a lifetime. Once missed, they might be gone for good.

I was going to apply for a job as the brand manager for GTI (Graduates to Internships) at Imperial College. You could say I was the right person for the job. I had the motivation, the experience, and the charisma needed to do the job. However, I kept procrastinating reading a book about GTI that would have enabled me to know more about them, a book that contained information necessary for me to do my job, a book that had been lying by my bed for weeks. On the day of the interview, I was unprepared. I knew nothing. Even though I was "the right person for the job", I didn't get the job. **It was a lesson learnt the hard way.**

Every time you procrastinate, you delay your future and the discovery of who you are. Putting off things now often leaves you with more things to do later. What have you not done that you were supposed to do? Procrastination delays visions coming to pass and goals being accomplished. By procrastinating, you miss your window of opportunity to do something important.

> every time you procrastinate, you delay your future and the discovery of *who you are.*

Procrastination really is the thief of time so stop leaving things to a later date.

With that, we come to the end of Day Five. Take some time to reflect on what you have learnt thus far.

day summary

- There are two categories of things that try to be obstacles to you discovering *who you are*: the enemy within (yourself) and people, places, situations and things.
- You create obstacles for yourself when you do any of the following:

  Have a disbelief in yourself. ***It is important to believe that you can do something if you really want to do it. Believe in yourself first, and then do it.***

  Are unwilling to solve the problems that most infuriate you. ***You were made to solve problems. Your anger determines what problems you should solve. Do not be afraid to solve problems. You were made for that purpose.***

  Procrastinate. ***Every time you procrastinate, you delay your future and the discovery of who you are. Do not procrastinate. Do today what you are meant to do today.***

day summary

say this prayer with me:

Father, thank You for the wisdom keys I have just received. Help me to overcome these obstacles by regaining a belief in myself, having the will and confidence to solve the problems that make me angry, and learning to do the right things at the right time.

My purpose is important to You, and this is the reason why You have given me this opportunity to change myself. Let this change my life.

Amen.

day six:

the enemy within part 2

Welcome to Day Six, where we conclude our discussion of the enemy within. We looked at three points yesterday:

- **disbelief in yourself,**
- **unwillingness to solve the problems that most infuriate you, and**
- **procrastination.**

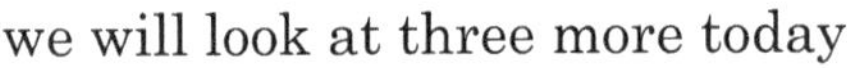

we will look at three more today

- **fear of failure**
- **past failures**
- **satisfaction in what you have already accomplished**

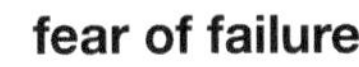

fear of failure

Fear is a big hindrance in any situation, but fear of failure is the most dangerous. The reason for this is that **it traps you in a snare so strong that it stops you from ever starting to succeed or discovering *who you are.*** Not doing something that you should because of the fear of failure is to fail before ever starting.

not doing something which you should, is to fail at it without ever starting.

People who fear failure do so because they have a disbelief in their own abilities, or they are overwhelmed by the size of their dream or vision–or the task at hand.

One of the things that I have always believed in is dreaming big. The problem with dreaming big, however, is the fact that sometimes the size of the dream can be overwhelming. This is very similar to disbelieving in yourself because they share the same origin: fear.

Having ambitious dreams can often lead to a **fear of tackling the next big thing.** You may doubt your abilities and fear to moving forward. To go forward might take some time and encouragement from those around you who believe in you and know your capabilities. You should never be afraid of the next level or challenge.

having ambitious dreams can often lead to a fear of tackling the next big thing.

The fear of failure limits your capability to discover *who you are.*

You should never fear failure because failure is not necessarily a bad thing. Let me explain.

If you fail at something, you are meant to learn from it. The most successful people in the world don't fear failure and have probably failed more times than you. Have you ever heard the saying "Nothing ventured, nothing gained"? The most successful people know (and so should you) **that you are not measured by your failures but by your successes.**

I have a game on my phone that shows the percentage of wins out of the number of games played. If you were to lose three in a row and give up, you would have a 0% win rate. However, if you were to lose twenty times but win forty times, you would have a 66.7% win rate. What is my point? Answer this question: Who has lost the most? Of course, the person with twenty losses. Who has won the most? Also the person with twenty losses. You can't be afraid to fail because life is not measured by how many times you fail but by how many times you win.

The fear of failure is the most crippling disease. When you fear failing at the next level, you never venture into it.

Try, try, try, and try again. Sometimes you have to fight to get through life. Just because you think that you are going to lose doesn't mean you should stop.

Would South Africa now have its independence if Nelson Mandela and the ANC (African National Congress) had folded at the prospects of facing the apartheid government, an entity that seemed far stronger and was more advanced in resources and technology? Even after being imprisoned with a life sentence, when some would consider themselves failures, Mandela made more or an impact inside prison than he did from the outside because there he started negotiations for peace. Twenty-seven years in prison could have destroyed that man or his vision, but he kept going. He overcame the odds and his limitations.

past failures

Continuing with the theme of failure, bad past experiences often colour people's perception of the present.

For example, perhaps a woman was hurt so badly in the past that she now refuses to see anything in men but the man that hurt her. Her past failure is governing her present life.

One thing you should know is that you should never be afraid to fail. No one wants to be a failure, but failing can teach you a lot of valuable lessons.

If you want to be the best at something, until you become the best at that thing, you are failing at being the best at that thing. But the day you become the best, you are crowned with success. It is your persistence that brings you to that point. What this means is that you will only fail at what you allow yourself to fail at.

To quote Thomas Edison when he was faced with failure before inventing the light bulb, **"I have not failed; I have just found ten thousand ways that it won't work".** And as Henry Ford said, **"Failure is only the opportunity to start again more intelligently".**

Some failures in life are necessary.

some failures in life are necessary.

I feel that I often failed at being an artist. However, if I had succeeded I might have been an artist and not be an author, and this book would never have been written. You would not be getting this information, and many lives would not be changed simply because I succeeded at something that I was not meant to succeed at. Please understand that there is nothing wrong with succeeding in things that are not your calling. In my case, though, I had a real passion for art and would do nothing but paint or draw for weeks. If I were an artist now, I would not be sitting here typing these words. Instead, I would be somewhere painting or drawing.

Thinking of a past failure can often hinder you just as much as other people reminding you of it. Perhaps you failed in the past at being a good person, but now you have changed. However, your friends who knew you when you were bad may constantly remind you of who you used to be. It is easy to be discouraged by their words and revert back to your old self. Don't do it.

> people will talk about your past failures; what you need to do is stop talking about it too.

People will talk about your past failures, and you can't control that. What you can do is stop talking about them. This was a hard lesson for me to learn because I would always talk about things I did or used to do as if I missed them.

Having failed in the past doesn't make you a failure. "Failure is an event, not a person", says Pastor Matthew Ashimolowo. To let a past failure imprison you is folly. Do not let your past rob you of your future. Learn from your mistakes, and don't make them again.

satisfaction in what you have already accomplished

"Until you hate where you are, you will never move forward". Satisfaction is one of the greatest foes you will ever face.

> "until you hate where you are, you will never move forward".

I used to go to the gym very infrequently. In fact, I hardly ever worked out. I would start but then stop. I would start because I saw people who have good builds. I wanted to have that, but when I started getting into shape, I would get content with what I saw and stop exercising. Such is the way of human nature.

We are creatures whose very nature tells us to adapt. When you adapt to something, you get used to it; when you get used to something you can tolerate it; when you can tolerate it, you can't change it; and when you stop changing, you get satisfied.

> we are creatures whose very nature tells us to adapt.

Satisfaction stops us from growing. When you are satisfied with good, you can never be great. **That is what satisfaction is–the difference between being good and being great.** The greatest people were never satisfied with the small victories that they achieved in life because they always saw the bigger picture.

> when you are satisfied with good, you can never be great.

Now what is really wrong with being satisfied? Isn't it good to be satisfied with what we have? At least, that is what a lot of us have been told. Others may think you are greedy when you are not content with what you have.

When I ask you not to be satisfied, I didn't ask you to be greedy. If you are satisfied with getting C's or D's at school, you will never get A's. Even if you are satisfied with a B, you will never push yourself to get an A. Is it greedy to want an A instead of a B?

When you get satisfied with where you are, you stop pushing. When you stop pushing, you stop aiming higher. This cuts you off from your full potential, as well as your full purpose and discovering *who you are.*

Satisfaction will only make you settle for less than you are really worth. You need to keep reaching if you ever want to accomplish fully what you were born to do.

We have come to the end of Day Six. Next, we will take a look at external enemies to discovering who you are: people, places, situations, and things. Take some time to reflect on what you have just read.

day summary

- There are two categories of obstacles to discovering *who you are*: the enemy within (yourself) and (other) people, places, situations, and things.
- You create obstacles for yourself when you do any of the following:

  Fear the act of failing: ***The fear of failing stops you for tackling the next thing and stops you from discovering who you are. Never fear failure because failure is not necessarily bad.***

  Focus on your past failures: ***Never let past failures stop you from doing something new. Some failures in life are necessary.***

  Become satisfied with where you are or what you have done in life: ***The biggest enemy to finding your purpose is satisfaction. It makes you settle for less than you are worth. Don't be satisfied but push on.***

say this prayer with me:

Father, Thank You for the wisdom keys I have just received. Help me to overcome these obstacles by rising above my fear of failure and gaining ambition for my purpose. Help me not let failures that happened in the past hold me in the past, and do not let me be satisfied with small successes.

My purpose is important to You and this is the reason You have given me this opportunity to change myself. Let this change my life.

Amen.

day seven:

people, places, situations, and things

You are your first enemy, so I have taken two days to explain why. However, you do have things external to yourself and out of your immediate control that try to oppose your purpose. These things I have broken down into the following:

- **family and friends**
- **being in the wrong place**
- **limitations**
- **giants, foes, and obstacles**
- **discouragement**

family and friends

One of the most terrible reasons why people never become *who they are* is because of their families and friends. These same people, the ones who are meant to cheer you on and help you get yourself on track, end up pulling you off your track.

There are many types of families and friends, and not all of them act in this fashion. The scary thing is that most of them do.

Have you ever met the family of someone with an extraordinary talent or gift? Imagine that person was not the first-born child of the family but the youngest. How do you suppose his or her older siblings would react to the younger sibling's successes in life? Would they be happy? In a lot of families, instead of being happy for their sibling they become jealous, angry, or bitter.

You, too, may have a younger brother or sister trying to impress the rest of your family with their gifts, always talking about their successes, sometimes just to get some attention. The older ones, on the other hand, may see this as an attempt to rub it in their faces, hence the anger and bitterness. This can often lead to disastrous events that can, and in most cases do, rob the younger one of their future and purpose.

In the Bible, Joseph is the second to the last born of boys in his family, and he had a dream that his brothers and parents would bow to him. His brothers hated him already because Joseph was a good boy and his father's favourite child. Now he would rule over them as well? When he told them of his dream, they hated him even more. Even his father rebuked him.

In an attempt to rob him of his future, his brothers framed his death and sold him as a slave to Egypt. Although it caused him many difficulties, their actions did not rob him but actually aided him because Joseph had a strong faith in his future and trust in his God.

As you can see, your family can rob you of your dream and vision out of jealousy. The same can be said about your friends. Friends and family can even discourage you from doing what you want in life, or they can remind you of your past failures or the kind of person you used to be. They can also point out of the difficulties you may face and discourage you from going through with your plans out of love or, even worse, disbelief in your abilities.

> your family can rob you of your dream and vision out of jealousy. the same can be said about your friends.

The reason why friends and family have such a huge impact on us and the way we see ourselves is because we see them as the people who should stand by us through thick and thin; the people we think should always encourage us; the people we think know us; the people we think we know. But as one of my mentors always says, **"Your family is the group of people that God sent you to prepare you for your future. If you can survive your family, then you can overcome any enemy ".**

Friends whom have known you for a long time can sometimes remind you of your beginnings in an attempt to humble you, to remind you of who you were in the past, or simply to belittle you. Remember, though, that every stage of your life was there to teach you one life lesson or another. Bringing up reminders of past mistakes is not right, especially when the person did not know who he or she was at the time. The person has already learnt that lesson. If you are constantly reminding someone of past mistakes, stop!

However, the worst way your friends and family prevent you from discovering *who you are* is when they say *no*.

the worst way in which your friends and family prevent you from discovering *who you are,* is when they say no.

If you are from West Africa, you should be able to relate to this. Parents only want their children to become doctors, lawyers, engineers, accountants, or businesspeople. To them, there are no other occupations worth pursuing. In their eyes, they are being good parents by doing this. I am not saying they are being bad parents, but they can also rob you of your destiny in an attempt to make you conform.

As I said earlier, these problems do not apply to all families or friends. There are those who encourage and support your decisions. **There are also those who say no and are right because they know better and are trying to steer you in the right direction. The only way to know the difference is through a close relationship with God and constant guidance from Him.** Although friends and families can be a problem, they can also be your greatest asset. Through their encouragement and support.

being in the wrong place

Where you are–this is just as important as *who you are. Where you are* determines who sees you. *Where you are* determines whom you see. It determines who talks to and influences you. It determines whom you talk to.

Discovering where you are meant to be is as life changing as discovering *who you are. Where you are* meant to be will change from time to time.

In agriculture, it is a well-known fact that the environment and the soil that a seed is planted in is just as important as the seed that is being planted. If the right seed is planted in the wrong environment, it will not grow. You have to be careful in deciding where you live, where you go to school, and where you hang spend your free time.

being in the wrong place

Discovering *who you are* also depends on *where you are.*

I often wonder if I would have taken the initiative to place myself in a position of leadership if I had not attended Imperial College. I attribute my new found appreciation for responsibility and leadership to the fact that I was pushed into being the first-year representative at my University's Afro Caribbean Society. Because of this experience, I was not afraid to undertake other visions that required the same if not greater levels of commitment.

Everyone you meet is important in defining and sculpting the person you become, but you have to be in the right place to meet the right people. People see qualities in you that define *who you are,* and having the right person see the right qualities in you is very important.

What you may need to fulfil your purpose may not reside in you but in the person beside you. Having the right person beside you comes from being in the right place.

i find that what you may need to fulfil your purpose may not reside in you but in the person beside you. having the right person beside you comes with being in the right place.

On the other hand, being around the wrong people and being in the wrong place will numb your sense of purpose and will limit the level of vision and encouragement that you receive. Being in the wrong place can stop your vision regardless of how good the seed is–the seed being you.

The wrong place can often be a place that seems good to human eyes.

Imagine if Moses stayed in Pharaoh's palace in Egypt instead of going into the wilderness. In the palace, he was safe and rich and had authority, but he would never have come to know God as well as he did if he had stayed. He would have forfeited his destiny and his purpose. It just goes to show that some things happen in life that on the surface appear bad but work for good in the end. Where are you now, in the wrong place or in the right place?

Know that sometimes the right place can seem an unlikely place for you to be.

limitations

I have seen wonderful people not realise their potential because of self-imposed limitations. I cannot conceive of some of the excuses people use to explain away why they are not good enough: I am not good enough because I am black; because I am a woman; because I am too young; because I am too old; because I am disabled.

We always seem to have a reason why we have not done something that we should have done. We always seem to have an excuse for our failures in life. We become our own biggest obstacle because we refuse to accept responsibility for our actions. We choose not to face the real problem, which is our self-imposed limitations but instead use them as excuses for failure. We cripple ourselves, our dreams, and our purpose.

> we always seem to have an excuse for our failures in life. we become our own biggest obstacle because we refuse to accept responsibility for our actions.

Does this sound like you? You may prefer to make an excuse for why you are not doing well rather than facing the problem.

The place you live or your race can be limitations, but your success is determined by how you overcome those limitations. **Focusing on your limitations will only set you up for failure.** You have already failed before you begin.

I have a student who uses the fact that he has dyslexia as his cushion. He is a bright kid, but he accepts the fact that he has dyslexia and doesn't try to face his problem. Dyslexia has become his limitation.

Dyslexia is a learning disorder. It doesn't mean you can't learn. It just means that you learn differently.

I, too, have symptoms of this disorder. In school, teachers could not understand why a bright kid like me would do well on some assessments and badly on others in the same subject. I thought that I was just not as smart as everyone else. It was not until I started doing my A-levels that I really started to believe in myself. I overcame my limitations.

If you were created to do something, where you come from, your gender, your race, and your school will not matter. **Just because you didn't start with a silver spoon in your mouth doesn't mean that you can't finish with a golden one.**

A very real limitation that people face is the lack of provision or what seems like a lack of provision.

Provision means arrangements, the care taken for what may happen, or the conditions for an event to occur. The word provision comes from two words: *pro* and *vision*. One definition of the word *pro* means *before*, so ***provision* means what you do before the vision, or the arrangements made before a vision.** Another definition of the word *pro* means *for*, so ***provision* also means what you do for your vision, or the arrangements made for a vision to occur.** Both definitions say the same thing.

A lot of people have a plan or vision but never seem to make provision for them. Then they wonder why the vision or plan never takes off.

Planning and timing are the keys to a lot of great success stories. Doing the right thing at the wrong time can be just as disastrous as doing the wrong thing.

so "provision" also means what you do for your vision; the arrangements made for a vision to occur.

Have you ever heard the saying, "If you fail to prepare, be prepared to fail"? There is a lot of sense in that statement. Preparation and planning are as essential to the success of any vision as goal setting. Without proper planning, you leave your success to chance.

Provision also concerns your readiness to move into another stage or a higher level financially, academically, or emotionally, your readiness to move on to the next level of your vision and your purpose.

Sometimes people try to rush their success by trying to move into the next level of their purpose prematurely. In almost all cases, they end up falling flat on their backs. As one of my friends would always say to me whenever I told her about my dreams and plans, "You will finish on time". That is what we all should aim for–**finishing on time.** There is no point rushing into something you are not ready for. A lot of people fail because they do that.

Morever, you can't live on a level that you didn't fight to attain. Imagine that a bird that normally flies at a 100 feet was suddenly made to fly at 400 feet. It would likely fall out of the sky. Until you learn the lesson of the next level, you can't live there.

Have you ever heard the saying, **"How you got in**

the door is how you will stay in the room"? What that means is that if you cheated to get in, then you will have to cheat to stay in. If you worked hard to get in, then you will have to work hard to stay in. You can't attain a level that you are not ready for, or you will not be able to do the work to keep yourself there.

> what that means is that if you cheated to get in, then you will have to cheat to stay in; if you worked hard to get in, then you will have to work hard to stay in.

Inadequate provision is sometimes not your fault. Imagine that you are accepted into a prestigious university but could not afford to pay the fees, so you settled for a lesser university, or worse, you got the grades to go to university but could not afford to go at all, so you give up your dreams. However, if it is part of your purpose to be something or to go somewhere, it will happen. There will have to be a way.

Pastor Matthew Ashimolowo, Senior Pastor of KICC (Kingsway International Christian Centre), one of the fastest growing churches in Europe and one of the biggest in the UK, first tried to be a pastor in the USA. He failed at this because his application for a visa was denied. If he had succeeded, there would have been no KICC. Thousands of lives would not have been changed by his messages, and this book would probably have been never written. All these things came to pass because a seeming failure became a success.

If there is no provision, you have the wrong vision. Search for your provision, and if there is none, maybe you need to look into changing your vision. **However, don't let the lack of provision rob you of your purpose and the discovery of *who you are.***

> if there is no provision then you have the wrong vision.

The lack of provision can make you believe that you were not meant to do something that is in your purpose to do. You may think that because you lack financial means or skill that you were not meant to achieve your goal.

What is limiting you? What have you been using as your excuse or cushion for failure? How can you overcome it?

giants, foes, and obstacles

Sometimes we come up against great odds that make us want to give up on our dreams. These odds can be academic, financial, social, or physical. I have broken them down into three categories: giants, foes, and obstacles.

Giants are large obstructions in front of us that prevent us from reaching or attaining our goals. Giants are obstructions that we have to fight and destroy in order to achieve our goals and accomplish our purpose.

People tend to run away from giants or be so overwhelmed by them that they are defeated before they even start fighting. Giants are placed in front of your purpose for a reason. What you can't possess on your own merits you are not ready for!

Sometimes people get a lot of money quickly and spend it almost as fast as they got it. **Most of the people who win the lottery never make more money than they win, and a lot of them still go broke.** The reason for this is that they were not ready for that level of riches. They fought no giant, so they learnt no lesson.

Defeating a giant makes you feel like you can do anything. It builds up your confidence.

> giants come in all shapes and sizes. they are meant to be defeated–you must fight them.

Giants come in all shapes and sizes. They are meant to be defeated–you must fight them. Any giant you don't fight and you try to get by will lead you away from or prevent you from walking into your purpose.

"Giants equal promotions". The level and size of the giant you fight determines the level and size of the promotion you get.

David was a boy anointed to be king over Israel. He had to kill the giant to come into the king's sight and also win the people's favour. He knew his weapon (the slingshot), he knew his skills, he knew his past victories (over the bear and lion), he knew his destiny, and he knew his God. Shepherd David grew up to be King David by overcoming obstacles, giants, and foes (including

King Saul). He became a man of battle and the protector of Israel. **However, before all this he was a shepherd in the back wood of nowhere, *training* until he was ready to defeat his giant.**

The skills you have now are what you will use to overcome your giants, obstacles, and foes. *Train* well and be ready to fight when the time comes.

Obstacles are obstructions that can be by passed, crossed over, or passed through.

> the way an obstacle is handled depends on the size, shape, and package in which it comes.

The way an obstacle is handled depends on the size, shape, and package in which it comes.

Obstacles could be a teacher who doesn't like you, a school that is prejudiced against your race, or a society that thinks little of you. Some obstacles must be lived through while others can be avoided. Sometimes you must live through certain things to gain knowledge and wisdom from your experience.

I am dyslexic, and because of this I can relate to other dyslexics. I have been in private schools and a state-owned school or two. I know what the environments are like, so I can relate to people from both kinds of schools. I have experienced very high levels of racism, and for this reason I am very tolerant of people's racial prejudice and feel no animosity toward anyone of a different race.

A foe is anyone or anything that is trying to stop you from achieving your purpose or goal. A foe destroys the influence you have on people in your presence or absence. We have all had enemies before, those who just don't like us and let us know it. There are people who will simply stand in your way to frustrate you and make you want to give up.

> foes are anything or person who is trying to stop you from achieving your purpose or goal.

In school, one boy tried his best to sabotage my artwork just because he didn't like me. He made me lose a few marks over the years, but he also made me learn a few lessons, as well. I know people won't always like me, and that is a price I have to pay for striving towards excellence. However, I can't allow that to stop me from achieving my goals, and neither should you.

I have met people who stopped doing something they loved because their "enemies", who were sometimes their friends, told them to stop. It is always a shame to see that, but it happens. You have to be strong and learn to overcome your enemies. **Some enemies are meant to be fought. Others are meant to be endured as they won't always be around you. You may find that some can be avoided completely.**

> some enemies are meant to be fought. others are meant to be endured as they won't always be around you. you may find that some can be avoided completely.

Life has taught me through my experiences and obstacles. Yes, giants may get in the way, obstacles may slow you down, and foes may try to stop you, but you must realise where you are going and keep your focus. Even after overcoming those giants and obstacles, there is something else not so obvious that hinders people.

discouragement

Discouragement is yet another crippler of dreams. It can come at anytime and from the most unlikely of places or people. For example, your teachers or, parents may discourage you from pursuing a dream or vision because they feel that you can't do it.

Discouragement is dangerous because it is not just a case of self-doubt but a case of others not believing in you. These people might be the closest people to you, the ones you think know you and expect to stand by you. They could be your best friend or your brother or sister. They may tell you that you cannot or should not do something that is your calling or greatest ambition in life. Imagine if all my friends had told me not to write this book, that it was bad idea, and that no one would read it. You probably would not be reading this right now.

your teachers, even parents may discourage you from pursuing a dream or vision because they feel that you can't do it.

I used to believe that discouragement could only come when you were at your lowest point. **It is true that if you are**

not good at something or you are going through a low point, it is very easy to get discouraged and give up.

> discouragement is most dangerous when it attacks you after a fall.

However, discouragement is most dangerous when it attacks you after a fall, when you seem to be living the dream and then suddenly, without warning, it all goes terribly wrong. You feel like you have been kicked in the gut and that perhaps what you were doing was not worth it. You may even begin to think of yourself as a failure. Failure after success can be a devastating blow.

I heard the story of a student of one of my teaching colleagues who wanted to be a doctor. The only problem was that everyone considered this girl to be dumb. She was writing her A levels at the time, and it didn't seem as if she was going to make the grades she needed, which were three A's. She didn't.

At this point, she could have felt discouraged and just given up. No one believed in her, and no one expected her to succeed. However, she retook the paper and got slightly higher grades but still not high enough. She had already spent an extra year taking her A levels, but she went back again. Some people would never do that, taking A levels for four years! The next time around, though, she made the grade.

She ended up at Cambridge University studying medicine, graduated with a high grade, and is now a doctor. She failed, but she was not discouraged and kept going.

Sometimes life makes us feel that we should just give up on our dreams. Discouragement is always hard to face and often easy to give into.

To overcome discouragement, you need to surround yourself with the right people–"encouragers". These are people who have your back; people who believe in you; people who will stand by you no matter what.

These types of people are not easy to find, but they are out there. In order to bring them to you, you need to announce your dream, but be careful whom you talk to. Some people are dream killers. I have learnt to discern whom to tell what to. This ability of discernment came from the Holy Spirit and my constant relationship with God.

Life discourages you. People discourage you. We all have to live with this fact. **You can't rely on your friends alone. Even as people encourage you, you have to learn to encourage yourself.** This comes from **remembering *who you are*, your past successes, your vision, and the giants that you have defeated in the past.**

And so we have reached the end of Day Seven. I know it was a long day with a lot of information, some of which you may not have known before. I would like you to reflect on this day as I say a little prayer for you:

> *Heavenly Father, I know discovering who you are is a tough process, and there are obstacles put in place because the devil does not want us to get there. Please help this reader. He or she has taken the first step by reading this book. Use it as an instrument to aid in overcoming any obstacle. In Jesus's name I pray. Amen.*

day summary

- There are two categories of obstacles to you discovering *who you are*: the enemy within (yourself) and (other) people, places, situations, and things.
- Other people, places, situations and things create an obstacle for yourself:

  People: ***Your family and friends can rob you of your dream out of jealousy, love, or disbelief in your abilities. They hardly see you for what you are becoming. Rather, they see you for what you were. They can say no to what you want to do or what you want to become in an attempt to protect you or hinder you. However, your family and friends can be your greatest asset because they can encourage you and help you grow. In the end, they want you to succeed.***

  Places: ***Where you are determines who sees you. Who sees you determines who talks to you and whom you talk to. Who talks to you determines who you become. Be in the right place. The right place can often seem like the wrong place to everyone else, but seek the face of God in all things.***

Situations: ***Focusing on your limitations only sets you up for failure. Provision means planning and preparation, what you do before the vision or for the vision. Inadequate provision means you have to wait until you are ready. Be proactive by preparing and planning. Purpose is not rushed–you will finish on time. Do not force yourself into a level for which you are not ready as this can lead to failure.***

Things: ***You are meant to fight and destroy your giants, for doing so reveals the secret of who you are. Giants equal promotions. Obstacles must be overcome. Search for a solution for that obstacle. Ask for help, read books, look for someone who went through what you are going through, overcome. Foes can be defeated, endured, or avoided. Pray for wisdom to know what to do, and God will give you the strength to do it. Discouragement can cripple your dreams. Surround yourself with people who encourage you all the time, that is, the right friend(s). Don't worry when discouragement comes. Everyone gets discouraged no matter how many victories won.***

say this prayer with me:

Father, thank You for the wisdom keys I have just received. Help me to overcome these obstacles by rising above people, places, situations and things that try to hold me back from accomplishing all that you want me to achieve.

My purpose is important to You and this is the reason You have given me this opportunity to change myself. Let this change my life.

Amen.

day eight:

what to do next part 1

The failure of many of the books that try to help you find your purpose is that they work you through the first step but not the second or third steps in this book. Therefore, I wrote this section to help you apply what you have learnt. It is a question that many people ask: Now that I have this knowledge, what do I do with it.

I formed a five step programme that I call "APLSyR" (pronounced "apple-sir"):

- **accept**
- **plan**
- **learn**
- **surround yourself**
- **review**

We will spend the last three days on these.

accept

looking for and accepting your differences

> the only way to walk into your purpose is to accept the fact that you are different.

The only way to walk into your purpose is to accept the fact that you are different. Everyone finds it hard to do this because everyone wants to fit in. If you do not accept yourself for *who you are,* however, how do you expect anyone else to do the same?

> if you do not accept yourself for who you are how do you expect anyone else to do the same?

Accepting yourself for being different and living with that difference is the first step in moving away from a life of conformance. To conform is to do what everyone else is doing.

I am not asking you to be an anti conformist, but I am asking you to look for what you want. **Take time out to know *who you are.***

I have known people who derive their identity from someone else, from their friends, from their girlfriends, from their boyfriends, or from their parents. You need to be able to stand up and say *who you are.*

For the longest time, I was known to many people at church as Tega's brother or at school as Aghogho's brother, so much so that I would introduce myself as such, almost as if I didn't have a name. You may think it sad, but don't you know some people as so-and-so's friend or so-and-so's sister or brother? You may even be someone like that yourself.

You need to stop deriving your identity from someone else and discover *who you are.*

plan

plan your paths to reach your purpose

What does that mean? It means write down your purpose and lifetime goal. Plan the path that you will take to reach it.

> your purpose is a lifetime event and not just for tomorrow, next year or ten years from now.

Your purpose is a lifetime event and not just for tomorrow, next year, or ten years from now. What you were born to do will take your entire life. "The cost of a big dream, a small dream or no dream is your life".

The cost you will pay for the purpose that

you were born to achieve is your life. Your life, your time, and your abilities are the only things that you can exchange for the future that you want, the future you deserve.

You may say that you do not know your purpose yet. If so, I will ask you to dream and make a plan to achieve that dream.

Write down what you want to achieve by the time you die. Dream big, the bigger the better. Now ask yourself, "Can I achieve that?" If you can achieve it, how can you achieve it? If you can't achieve it, why can't you?

If you can do it, write down how you intend to do it with goals you set for yourself along the way, one-year goals, ten-year goals, twenty-year goals, and so on. Map out the path that you intend to take in order to achieve your dream and your purpose. Place the map somewhere you can access it on demand to measure your progress. Place the map where you can see it all the time, and let it motivate you.

For those of you who think you do not know how to dream, it is easy. Sit back and imagine yourself ten years from now looking back at all the things you have achieved. Picture them clearly: the year, the place, the day, the people, and the situation. Now write that down with all the details. Those are your dreams.

Instead of trying to achieve the greatest goal–your purpose–aim for the next step on your ladder. Once you have achieved that, aim for the next. You have the map laid out in front of you, so follow it. Sometimes you may have to change the path you take to reach the end, but never change the end.

> instead of trying to achieve the greatest goal–your purpose–aim for the next step on your ladder.

If you can't do it, ask yourself why. What are you doing, or rather not doing, that is stopping you from achieving your dream? How can you correct that?

Change yourself to make your dream a reality. The secret to your future success can be found in your daily routine.

> change yourself to make your dream a reality.

Some people might say that things do not always work out the way they plan. Sure, they don't always, but if you have a plan, all you have to do is to change it slightly to match the situation.

Planning out your life and putting the map in front of you creates the motivation that you need. All you have to do is read the map regularly and make corrections to it when and if needed. I do that to mine once every month.

Place a painting of what you want to be in front of you. Have that there all the time: a picture in your wallet, on the walls of you room, in a book that you always carry around with you.

Always have something with you that carries your future on it or in it. Do this so that even when you go slightly adrift from you purpose, you can always look at the picture and get back on track. The greatest motivation is your sense of purpose and the need to become *who you are.*

something for you to do:

What is your next step?

____

____

____

Can you achieve that now?

____

If not, why not?

____

____

____

What do you need to do in other to achieve that?

____

____

____

How soon can you do that?

____

____

____

learn

Learn from your experience and through your mistakes.

Everyday of your life is a training day for the next day. What you learn today use to improve tomorrow.

what you learn today, you must now use to improve tomorrow.

A great man once said that a day you spend not learning anything doesn't have a tomorrow but a longer today. In other words, if you don't learn anything today, you have not grown for tomorrow. What you have done is just extend the level that you are at by another day, so in fact it is just a longer today.

Whatever lesson that life teaches you today should be used tomorrow to solve a problem, used tomorrow to encourage you when you are down, used tomorrow as a reminder of your victories when you come up against an enemy that seems too big.

Speaking of enemies, just remember this: "The size of your giant is a prophecy of your reward" – Pastor Matthew Ashimolowo.

Before he fought Goliath, David reminded himself about the bear and the lion that he killed. His previous days had just been training days for what he was now doing.

Winston Churchill described his life before his great appointment as a preparation for what he was about to face. He believed that he could never fail, because he was in the purpose for which he was born.

---

every day is a training day

a day you spend not learning anything doesn't have a tomorrow but a longer today.

Take every experience in life as a training day for the next, but most important, learn. This requires you to go back to school.

When I say back to school, I don't mean "school" school. I mean the school of life. Life is a school, and it is always trying to teach you something. The problem is some of us are not learning. We have stopped learning or, worse, never started learning.

Life tries to teach us everything we need to know in order to survive in it. It may teach us on our own or through someone else, but more than any other way, life teaches us through our mistakes.

doing the same thing twice and expecting a different result is insanity.

As humans we make a lot of mistakes, but we are meant to learn from them. Doing the same thing twice and expecting a different result is insanity. You can't keep repeating the same approach and expect a different result.

Go back to school! Learn from your mistakes. It will help you to grow and to overcome the next set of problems you face.

I will pause here for today, and we will pick up the five-step programme tomorrow. Remember, **accept** who you are, **plan** to achieve your dreams and **learn** from your mistakes and experiences.

day summary

- “APLSyR” stands for Accept, Plan, Learn, Surround yourself, and Review.
- **Accept:** you are different from everyone else. You are unique, so look for what makes you different.
- **Plan:** in order to accomplish any vision or goal, you have to plan. Lay out a strategy and a direction in which to move. Put down as much as you can on paper.
- **Learn:** your experience and your mistakes are your teachers. What is life trying to teach you? What traps have you fallen into time and time again?

day nine:
what to do next part 2

Welcome to Day Nine. As this is the last day of reading, I wanted it to be a day of light reading. We will be looking at the last two steps in the five step programme:

- **surround yourself**
- **review**

surround yourself

This section gives you two powerful keys to enable you to overcome the obstacles that come with discovering your purpose:

- **surround yourself with encouragers**
- **surround yourself with your purpose**

surround yourself with encouragers

To find and stay in your calling requires a large amount of motivation. Maintaining all of this motivation on your own can be strenuous. **The most effective way to keep motivated in the first few weeks of discovering *who***

***you are* is to tell someone about the change in you and what you want to achieve.** Granted, this in itself requires courage, and you need to find the right person to confide in.

surround yourself with encouragers

When I first started the discovery of *who I am,* my best friend at the time stopped talking to me. **Certain people in your life will have to move on when you move up.** We were no longer a fit for each other, but I didn't see this at the time. Strained friendships can often lead people to abandon their pursuit of discovering *who they are,* but I stuck with it.

Now that I look back, I am actually glad that she decided to stop talking to me. It is hard to change yourself, and to have someone in your life who knew the old "you" can make the process of finding *who you are* even more challenging. Often these friends try to pull you back to where you were before your discovery. I later found a best friend in someone I had always known but never really knew.

He is my chief encourager, my number one helper, like a brother to me, and I trust him more than he will ever know. No, I am not talking about Jesus but a companion here on this earth. I tell him everything: every vision, every plan, every dream. I knew *who he was* before he did.

---

for all this motivation to come from you can be strenuous.

Finding someone like that is not easy and can't happen on its own. You have to ask God to show you the person or people who will stand by you through all things.

when you tell someone about your vision, they bug you and ask you about it until you do it.

When you tell the right person about your vision, they will bother you and ask you about it until you achieve it .

Telling people about your purpose helps to force you into your destiny and your future. Joseph told his brothers about his dream; Moses told the people his purpose; Samuel anointed David in the presence of his family. All these things helped to force them into the purposes that God had for them. **Anything hidden can be denied and nullified, so never be ashamed to declare what the Lord has shown you.**

Remember, the Bible does not say that bad things will not happen to you. It says that "all things work together … for good to those who love God and are called according to [His] design and purpose" (Romans 8:28, Amplified Bible). So when someone does something wrong toward you, like my best friend leaving me in my time of need–know that–**it all works together for good.**

something for you to do:

Who are your encouragers?

What can you do to appreciate them?

surround yourself with your purpose

You can only succeed at something that you make your obsession. Live it, eat it, and breathe it. Let every conversation you have and every friend you choose be based on this purpose and obsession. Let it consume your world until your name becomes synonymous with it.

> you can only succeed at something that you make your obsession.

When you think computers, you may think Microsoft (Bill Gates) and Dell (Michael Dell). When you think football, you think David Beckham, Thierry Henry, John Terry or Wayne Rooney. What do people think of when they think of you?

Make your purpose your obsession.

review

Although the section review is part of my five step programme, I have split it over two days, mainly because it is also what the final day is about.

the picture you paint

It is very easy to be led astray by what we think our purpose is in life. Sometimes we see something and jump in headfirst.

the picture you paint

if life were a mural and you were just painting one section only you would run into a lot of problems because you would have an incomplete painting.

When I began my discovery of *who I am,* I almost became a pastor. I wanted to become a pastor because of my gift for teaching and the "word of knowledge". This would have been a mistake Not that I will not be a pastor in years to come, but to be a pastor right now is not my purpose. If I were a pastor rather than an author, this book might have been just one sermon, and the information you are reading might never have gotten to you.

If life were a mural and you were just painting one section you would run into a lot of problems because you would have an incomplete painting. We have to be careful while we are walking in our purpose, painting the mural, not to pay so much attention to one gift that we let other gifts die.

> it is best for you to wait until you see the complete picture before you commit yourself to just one area of what you were called to do or to the wrong thing all together.

The key here is **balance.** You should never throw away your future for your today. It should be the other way round–**delayed gratification.**

Another way of looking at it is that you are a physical object or tool in life but don't know exactly what kind of tool you are when you arrive on earth. Your entire childhood is meant to be the time you try to find out what that purpose is. Let's say that you find out that you are meant to be a pair of scissors, and for that reason you start to cut garden hedges. However, you are not a pair of garden scissors but a pair of kitchen scissors. Trying to cut hedges would destroy your blades.

It is best for you to wait until you see the complete picture before you commit yourself to just one area of what you were called to do or end up doing the wrong thing all together.

I am going to say something that might shock you: education is not the only way to success. In fact education, in most cases, doesn't make you wealthy or give you an abundant life. Even if you were to give most of your attention to your academic gifts (like I used to) and try to see how far that would get you in life, you would most likely get just a J.O.B, which stands for "Just over Broke". That is what a job is.

Education will get you a job and could get you a very good job, mind you. In fact, if you are really lucky, it could make you rich. However, God didn't call you to this earth just to get a job. God didn't call you to this earth purely to do someone else's work.

however, god didn't call you to this earth just to get a job. god didn't call you to this earth purely to do someone else's work.

When you get a job, you are helping someone else achieve their dream, but you are not achieving yours. Go ahead and get a job, but don't get trapped in one. Jobs are great learning experiences and before I started my tutoring agency, I worked in three tutoring agencies and had at least three years of paid experience. I could not get that job if I were not academically gifted, but I have learned over the years that **academics are not difficult. Succeeding in life is.**

I am not saying that everyone should go into business. I can have a job in a good company that makes me feel fulfilled at the end of every day. If so, that job is no longer just a job–it has now become *work.* You can also have a job, come home every day, and do something else that fulfils you and your purpose. That thing then becomes your *work.* You need to *work* and not just have a job.

academics is not difficult, succeeding in life is.

Peter J. Daniels, a rags-to-riches multi-millionaire who never went to University and failed at school, once said, **"The cost of a big dream, a small dream or no dream is your life".**

We have come to the end of Day Nine, which is the end of the reading section. Keep in mind that this book will not discover who you are for you. It will help you to start asking yourself the right questions, to start thinking, to start acting, to start being, to start living, and to get you into the right mindset.

If you do not know *who you are,* you have not started living. The life you live now is not yours and is not **life until you discover a purpose to it. When will you start living?**

I left the most important obstacle to discovering who you are to the end. Many people try to discover who they are on their own–without the most vital element–God.

many people try to discover who they are on their own, without the most vital element – God.

You can't discover a purpose to your life without the Holy Spirit. You can't know the Holy Spirit without God the Father. You can't go to God the Father without going through Jesus Christ. You can't go through Jesus Christ if you don't know Him. **It all starts with you and the decisions you make.**

This is the most important decision that you will make

in your life. Do not take it lightly. If you do not know Jesus Christ, it is important that you do. I want you to say this simple prayer with me that will alter your life and your destiny forever. It is a prayer to accept Jesus Christ as your Lord and personal Saviour:

> *'Father, I am sorry for my sins. I know now that I can't live my life without You. Please forgive me for my sins. Jesus, come into my heart, come into my life. Help me to live my life for You. Amen.'*

Now you can begin your discovery of *who you are.* Search deep within yourself and search outside as well. Ask the Holy Spirit to guide you and lead you. Read this book again. And, finally, the best life manual of all is God's own word–the Bible–Read it!

I ask that you join your local church and tell them of your decision.

Day ten will help you review.

day summary

- "APLSyR" stands for Accept, Plan, Learn, Surround yourself and Review.
- **Surround yourself:** fill your life with encouragers and with your purpose. Make your purpose your obsession. Have people around you who say positive things about your life and your purpose.
- **Review:** take sometime to look at your life as a whole. What picture are you painting? What is missing? What do you need to improve?

day ten:

review

You have reached the final day of your journey. It has taken you ten days to get here, but it took me many years to be able to get you here. Thank you for travelling on this amazing journey with me. To finish off we will go through a complete review of what you have learnt.

the complete review

Go back to the "How to discover *who you are*" section and review all the answers that you wrote. Prayerfully meditate on your answers and begin to piece to together answers to the question *who are you?*

something for you to do:

Pray and ask for the Holy Spirit to guide you to discover who you are.

Who are you?

____

____

____

What is your life-long dream?

What are your dreams for the next twelve months? (Put dates on them).

January

February

March

April

May

June

July

August

September

October

November

December

What are your one-month goals?

Knowing that it is good to study around your purpose and passions, what are your reading goals?

What other goals will you need to set to achieve your purpose?

Who can you get to help you achieve your purpose?

What type of friends do you need to have?

____

____

____

What sort of mentor would you like to have?

____

____

____

Who can you talk to regularly about your purpose?

____

____

____

Finally, pray regularly about your purpose. You cannot achieve it without God.

www.ingramcontent.com/pod-product-compliance
Ingram Content Group UK Ltd.
Pitfield, Milton Keynes, MK11 3LW, UK
UKHW020140250726
13967UKWH00002B/774

9 781425 163747